Easy Cake Cookbook

50 Delicious Cake Recipes

By
BookSumo Press
All rights reserved

Published by
http://www.booksumo.com

ENJOY THE RECIPES?

KEEP ON COOKING WITH 6 MORE FREE COOKBOOKS!

Visit our website and simply enter your email address to join the club and receive your 6 cookbooks.

http://booksumo.com/magnet

https://www.instagram.com/booksumopress/

https://www.facebook.com/booksumo/

LEGAL NOTES

All Rights Reserved. No Part Of This Book May Be Reproduced Or Transmitted In Any Form Or By Any Means. Photocopying, Posting Online, And / Or Digital Copying Is Strictly Prohibited Unless Written Permission Is Granted By The Book's Publishing Company. Limited Use Of The Book's Text Is Permitted For Use In Reviews Written For The Public.

Table of Contents

Lemon Pudding Cake 7

Yellow Vanilla Cake 8

Holiday Cake 9

Pineapple, Orange, and Vanilla Yellow Cake 10

Fabulous Layered Cake 11

Sour Cream Dark Chocolate Cake 13

A Southern Cake 14

Moroccan Orange Cake 15

Easy Wedding Cake 16

American Unbaked Cake 17

A Comforting Cake 18

Old-Fashioned Cake 19

Strawberry Punch Cake 20

Gift Cake 21

Chocolate Coffee Cake 22

German Style Chocolate Cake 23

Buttermilk Chocolate Cake 25

Semi-Sweet Chocolate Cake 26

Cookout Cake 27

October's Cake 28

Alabama Inspired Cake 29

Cinnamon Fudgy Cake 31
Cheesecake Japanese Style 32
Maple Pecan Cheesecake 33
Delightful Cheesecake 34
Expresso Cheesecake 35
East Coast Style Cheesecake 36
Spanish Berry Cheesecake 37
Potluck Cake 39
Classic Cake 40
Super Moist Carrot Cake 41
Traditional Latin Cake 42
Surprisingly Crunchy Cake 43
Cocoa Cake 44
Rustic Cake 45
Artisanal Style Cake 46
Cinnamon Apple Cake 47
Raisins and Walnuts Cake 48
Lemony Lemon Cake 49
Louisiana Cajun Cake 50
Chocolate Cheesecake Irish Style 53
November's Cheesecakes 54
Party-Time Cheesecakes 55
Movie Time Cake 56

Outstanding Cake 57

A Cake For Couples 58

Elegant Mousse 59

Ethan's Favorite Cakes 60

Valentine's Day Cake 61

Special Summertime Mini Cakes 62

Traditional German Cake 63

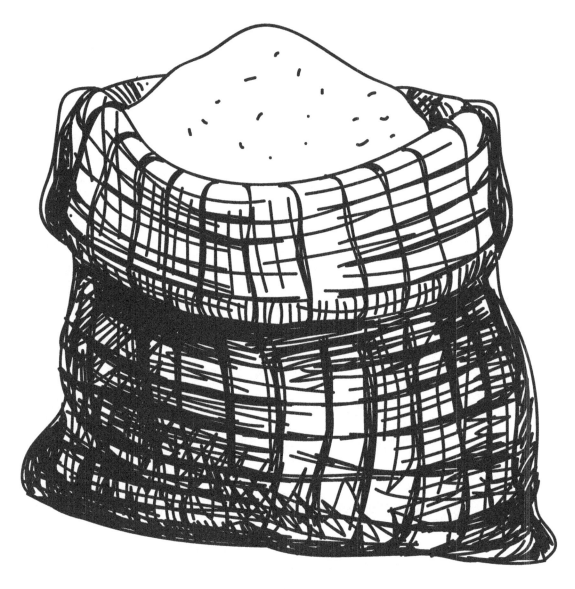

Lemon Pudding Cake

Prep Time: 30 mins
Total Time: 35 mins

Servings per Recipe: 12
Calories	425 kcal
Fat	13 g
Carbohydrates	74.1g
Protein	4.7 g
Cholesterol	73 mg
Sodium	441 mg

Ingredients

- 4 eggs
- 1 (3 oz.) package instant lemon pudding mix
- 1/3 C. vegetable oil
- 1 (18.25 oz.) package lemon cake mix
- 3/4 C. water
- 1/2 C. lemon juice
- 3 C. sifted confectioners' sugar
- 1/4 C. confectioners' sugar for dusting

Directions

1. Set your oven to 350 degrees F before doing anything else and grease and flour a bundt pan.
2. In a bowl, add the eggs and beat till thick.
3. Add the cake mix, pudding mix, oil and water and with an electric mixer, beat on medium speed for about 5 minutes.
4. Transfer the mixture into the prepared pan and cook in the oven for about 50 minutes or till a toothpick inserted in the center comes out clean.
5. Meanwhile for glaze in a mix together the 3 C. of the confectioner's sugar and lemon juice and heat till boiling.
6. Pour the hot glaze over the hot cake and keep aside for about 1 hour to cool.
7. Carefully, invert the cake over the serving plate.
8. Serve with a dusting of the confectioner's sugar.

YELLOW
Vanilla Cake

Prep Time: 30 mins
Total Time: 1 hr 30 mins

Servings per Recipe: 12
Calories 562 kcal
Fat 29.9 g
Carbohydrates 59.2g
Protein 5.6 g
Cholesterol 83 mg
Sodium 476 mg

Ingredients

1 C. chopped walnuts
1 (18.25 oz.) package yellow cake mix
1 (3.4 oz.) package instant vanilla pudding mix
4 eggs
1/2 C. water
1/2 C. vegetable oil
1/2 C. cranberry

1/2 C. butter
1/4 C. water
1 C. white sugar
1/2 C. apple juice

Directions

1. Set your oven to 325 degrees F before doing anything else and grease and flour a 10-inch bundt pan.
2. In the bottom of the prepared pan, spread the walnuts.
3. In a large bowl, mix together the pudding mix and cake mix.
4. Add the eggs, oil, 1/2 C. of the cranberry juice and 1/2 C. of the water and mix till well combined.
5. Transfer the mixture over walnuts evenly and cook in the oven for about 60 minutes or till a toothpick inserted in the center comes out clean.
6. For glaze in a pan, mix together the butter, 1 C. of the sugar and 1/4 C. of the water on medium heat.
7. Bring to a boil and boil for about 5 minutes, stirring continuously.
8. Remove from the heat and immediately, stir in the apple juice.
9. Remove the cake from the oven and keep aside for about 10 minutes.
10. Cot the top and sides of the cake with the glaze evenly.
11. Let the cake absorb the glaze completely, then again coat with the remaining glaze.

Holiday Cake

Prep Time: 30 mins
Total Time: 3 hrs 30 mins

Servings per Recipe: 12
Calories   681 kcal
Fat   31 g
Carbohydrates   87.6g
Protein   4.8 g
Cholesterol   83 mg
Sodium   457 mg

Ingredients

- 1 (18.25 oz.) package yellow cake mix
- 4 eggs
- 1 (3.3 oz.) package instant white chocolate pudding mix
- 1/2 C. cold water
- 1/2 C. vegetable oil
- 1/2 C. amaretto liqueur
- 1/4 tsp almond extract
- 1/2 C. butter
- 1/4 C. water
- 1 C. white sugar
- 1/2 C. amaretto liqueur
- 1 (16 oz.) package vanilla frosting
- 1/4 C. blanched slivered almonds

Directions

1. Set your oven to 350 degrees F before doing anything else and lightly, grease a 10-inch nonstick bundt pan.
2. In a large bowl, add the pudding mix, cake mix, 1/2 C. of the amaretto, oil, 1/2 C. of the cold water and almond extract and beat till well combined.
3. Transfer the mixture into the prepared pan and cook in the oven for about 45-60 minutes or till a toothpick inserted in the center comes out clean.
4. Meanwhile for glaze in a pan, mix together the butter, sugar, 1/4 C. water, and 1/2 C. amaretto and ring to a boil. Boil for about 10 minutes, stirring continuously.
5. Remove the cake from the oven and with a skewer make as many holes as possible into the cake.
6. Slowly, pour glaze over the top and sides of the warm cake and let it cool in the pan for at least 2 hours.
7. For topping lightly toast slivered almonds in the oven for about 5-10 minutes, stirring occasionally. Heat 1/4 C. of the prepared frosting in the microwave for about 10 seconds.
8. Transfer the cake on serving plate and drizzle with the softened frosting evenly.
9. Sprinkle the toasted almonds over the cake before frosting cools.

PINEAPPLE, Orange, and Vanilla Yellow Cake

Prep Time: 30 mins
Total Time: 9 hrs 55 mins

Servings per Recipe: 12
Calories 452 kcal
Fat 16.4 g
Carbohydrates 73.9 g
Protein 3.8 g
Cholesterol 22 mg
Sodium 465 mg

Ingredients

1 (18.25 oz.) package yellow cake mix
8 oz. cream cheese
1 1/2 C. confectioners' sugar
1 (20 oz.) can crushed pineapple with juice
2 (8 oz.) cans mandarin oranges, drained
1 (3.5 oz.) package instant vanilla pudding mix
1 (8 oz.) container frozen whipped topping, thawed

Directions

1. Mix and bake the cake mix as per package instruction for 2 (8-9-inch) round layers.
2. Keep aside the layers to cool and then split each layer in half so as to have 4 layers.
3. In a large bowl, add the cream cheese and beat till soft.
4. Slowly, mix in the confectioners' sugar.
5. Add the pineapple with juice and the drained mandarin oranges, reserving about 5 mandarin orange slices and mix till well combined.
6. Mix in the dry pudding mix and fold in the whipped topping.
7. Arrange one cake layer onto a cake plate cut side up.
8. Spread frosting over the layer and place another layer cut side down on the first one.
9. Top with the frosting.
10. Repeat till all the layers are used, spreading all the frosting on top and sides of cake.
11. Garnish with the reserved mandarin orange slices.
12. Refrigerate for overnight before serving.

Fabulous Layered Cake

Prep Time: 5 mins
Total Time: 2 hrs

Servings per Recipe: 12
Calories   465 kcal
Fat   28.9 g
Carbohydrates   46.3g
Protein   4.4 g
Cholesterol   78 mg
Sodium   309 mg

Ingredients

Cake:
1 (18.25 oz.) package moist white cake mix
1 tsp instant coffee powder
1/4 C. coffee
1 tbsp coffee flavored liqueur
Filling:
1 (8 oz.) container mascarpone cheese
1/2 C. confectioners' sugar
2 tbsp coffee flavored liqueur

Frosting:
2 C. heavy cream
1/4 C. confectioners' sugar
2 tbsp coffee flavored liqueur
Garnish:
2 tbsp unsweetened cocoa powder
1 (1 oz.) square semisweet chocolate

Directions

1. Set your oven to 350 degrees F before doing anything else and grease and flour 3 (9-inch) cake pans.
2. Mix the cake mix according to package directions.
3. Divide two thirds of the mixture between 2 pans.
4. In the remaining mixture, stir in the instant coffee and transfer into the third pan.
5. Cook in the oven for about 20-25 minutes or till a toothpick inserted in the center comes out clean.
6. Let the cakes cool in the pans for about 10 minutes, then turn out onto a wire rack and cool completely.
7. In a cup, mix together the brewed coffee and 1 tbsp of the coffee liqueur and keep aside.
8. For the filling in a small bowl, add the mascarpone, 1/2 C. of the confectioners' sugar and 2 tbsp of the coffee liqueur and with an electric mixer set on low speed, beat till just smooth.
9. Cover with plastic wrap and refrigerate.
10. For the frosting in a medium bowl, add the cream, 1/4 C. of the confectioners' sugar and

2 tbsp of the coffee liqueur and with an electric mixer set on medium-high speed, beat till stiff.
11. Fold 1/2 C. of the cream mixture into the filling mixture.
12. For assembling, place one plain cake layer on a serving plate and with a thin skewer, poke holes in cake, about 1 inch apart.
13. Place one third of the reserved coffee mixture over the cake, then spread half of the filling mixture.
14. Top with the coffee-flavored cake layer and poke the holes in the cake.
15. Place another third of the coffee mixture over the second layer and spread with the remaining filling.
16. Top with the remaining cake layer and poke holes in the cake.
17. Place the remaining coffee mixture on top.
18. Spread the frosting on the sides and top of the cake.
19. Place cocoa in a sieve and lightly dust over the cake and garnish with the chocolate curls.
20. Refrigerate the cake for at least 30 minutes before serving.
21. (To make the chocolate curls, use a vegetable peeler and run it down the edge of the chocolate bar.)

Sour Cream Dark Chocolate Cake

Prep Time: 30 mins
Total Time: 2 hrs

Servings per Recipe: 12
Calories   528 kcal
Fat   26.4 g
Carbohydrates   66 g
Protein   6.1 g
Cholesterol   63 mg
Sodium   498 mg

Ingredients

- 1 (18.25 oz.) package dark chocolate cake mix
- 1 (3.9 oz.) package instant chocolate pudding mix
- 1 (16 oz.) container sour cream
- 3 eggs
- 1/3 C. vegetable oil
- 1/2 C. coffee flavored liqueur
- 2 C. semisweet chocolate chips

Directions

1. Set your oven to 350 degrees F before doing anything else and grease and flour a bundt pan.
2. In a large bowl, add the pudding mix, cake mix, eggs, sour cream, oil and coffee liqueur and beat till well combined.
3. Transfer the mixture into the prepared pan and cook in the oven for about 60 minutes or till a toothpick inserted in the center comes out clean.
4. Cool for about 10 minutes in the pan, then turn out and cool completely on wire rack.

A SOUTHERN Cake

Prep Time: 15 mins
Total Time: 8 hrs 50 mins

Servings per Recipe: 24
Calories 288 kcal
Fat 14.6 g
Carbohydrates 36.6g
Protein 3.5 g
Cholesterol 42 mg
Sodium 190 mg

Ingredients

1 (18.25 oz.) package white cake mix
3 eggs
1/3 C. vegetable oil
1 C. water
1/2 tsp coconut extract
1 (14 oz.) can sweetened cream of coconut

1 (14 oz.) can sweetened condensed milk
1 C. heavy whipping cream
1 tbsp white sugar
1 C. flaked coconut

Directions

1. Set your oven to 350 degrees F before doing anything else and grease and flour a 13x9-inch cake pan.
2. In a large bowl, add the cake mix, eggs, oil, water and coconut flavoring and beat for about 2 minutes.
3. Transfer the mixture into the prepared pan and cook in the oven for about 30 minutes or till a toothpick inserted in the center comes out clean.
4. In a medium bowl, add the coconut cream and sweetened condensed milk and stir till smooth.
5. Remove the cake from the oven and with a fork, poke holes.
6. Place the milk mixture over the cake, allowing it to soak into the cake.
7. Refrigerate for several hours or overnight.
8. In a large bowl, add the cream and beat till soft peaks form.
9. Add the sugar and beat till stiff.
10. Spread over cooled cake and serve with a sprinkling of the flaked coconut.

Moroccan Orange Cake

Prep Time: 30 mins
Total Time: 2 hrs

Servings per Recipe: 12
Calories   410 kcal
Fat   19.8 g
Carbohydrates   55g
Protein   4.2 g
Cholesterol   73 mg
Sodium   443 mg

Ingredients

1 (18.25 oz.) package yellow cake mix
1 (3 oz.) package instant lemon pudding mix
3/4 C. orange juice
1/2 C. vegetable oil
4 eggs
1 tsp lemon extract
1/3 C. orange juice
2/3 C. white sugar
1/4 C. butter

Directions

1. Set your oven to 450 degrees F before doing anything else and grease and flour a bundt pan.
2. In a large bowl, mix together the cake mix and pudding mix.
3. Make a well in the center and add in 3/4 C. of the orange juice, oil, eggs and lemon extract and eat on low speed till well combined.
4. Scrape the bowl, and now, beat on medium speed for about 4 minutes.
5. Transfer the mixture into the prepared pan and cook in the oven for about 50-60 minutes or till a toothpick inserted in the center comes out clean.
6. Let the cake cool in the pan for about 10 minutes, then turn out onto a wire rack and cool completely.
7. In a pan, add 1/3 C. of the orange juice, sugar and butter on medium heat and cook for about 2 minutes.
8. Drizzle over the cake.

EASY
Wedding Cake

Prep Time: 10 mins
Total Time: 1 hr 5 mins

Servings per Recipe: 20
Calories	211 kcal
Fat	6.6 g
Carbohydrates	35.3g
Protein	2.9 g
Cholesterol	5 mg
Sodium	275 mg

Ingredients

1 (18.25 oz.) package white cake mix
1 C. all-purpose flour
1 C. white sugar
3/4 tsp salt
1 1/3 C. water
1 C. sour cream
2 tbsp vegetable oil

1 tsp almond extract
1 tsp vanilla extract
4 egg whites

Directions

1. Set your oven to 325 degrees F before doing anything else and grease and flour a 13x11-inch cake pan.
2. In a bowl, mix together the white cake mix, flour, sugar, and salt.
3. Add the sour cream, egg whites, vegetable oil, water, almond and vanilla extracts and beat with an electric mix on low for about 4 minutes.
4. Transfer the mixture into the prepared pan and cook in the oven for about 25 minutes or till a toothpick inserted in the center comes out clean.
5. Allow to cool before frosting.

American Unbaked Cake

Prep Time: 30 mins
Total Time: 1 hr

Servings per Recipe: 10
Calories	827 kcal
Fat	44.6 g
Carbohydrates	101.5g
Protein	9.9 g
Cholesterol	56 mg
Sodium	896 mg

Ingredients

- 1/2 C. butter, softened
- 1 (8 oz.) package cream cheese, softened
- 1/2 C. confectioners' sugar
- 2 (3.5 oz.) packages instant vanilla pudding mix
- 3 1/2 C. milk
- 1 (12 oz.) container frozen whipped topping, thawed
- 32 oz. chocolate sandwich cookies with crème filling

Directions

1. In a food processor, add the cookies and pulse till chopped finely.
2. In a bowl, add the cream cheese, butter and sugar and beat till well combined.
3. In another large bowl add the milk, pudding and whipped topping and mix till well combined.
4. Add the cream cheese mixture and mix till well combined.
5. In a flower pot, place the ingredients in the layers, starting with cookies then cream mixture.
6. Repeat the layers and refrigerate to chill until ready to serve.
7. Add artificial flower and trowel.

A COMFORTING
Cake

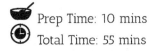
Prep Time: 10 mins
Total Time: 55 mins

Servings per Recipe: 24
Calories   155 kcal
Fat   6.4 g
Carbohydrates   24.3g
Protein   1.2 g
Cholesterol   11 mg
Sodium   171 mg

Ingredients

2 (16 oz.) cans peaches in heavy syrup
1 (18.25 oz.) package yellow cake mix
1/2 C. butter
1/2 tsp ground cinnamon, or to taste

Directions

1. Set your oven to 375 degrees F before doing anything else.
2. In the bottom of a 13x9-inch pan, place the peaches.
3. Spread the dry cake mix over the peaches and press down firmly.
4. Cut butter into small pieces and place on top of cake mix and sprinkle with the cinnamon evenly.
5. Cook in the oven for about 45 minutes.

Old-Fashioned Cake

Prep Time: 40 mins
Total Time: 1 hr 20 mins

Servings per Recipe: 24
Calories   282 kcal
Fat   15.7 g
Carbohydrates   34.1g
Protein   2.8 g
Cholesterol   31 mg
Sodium   275 mg

Ingredients

- 1 (18.25 oz.) package yellow cake mix
- 1 (3.4 oz.) package instant vanilla pudding mix
- 1 (3.4 oz.) package instant butterscotch pudding mix
- 4 eggs
- 1 C. water
- 1 C. vegetable oil
- 1 C. packed brown sugar
- 1 tbsp ground cinnamon
- 1 C. chopped walnuts

Directions

1. Set your oven to 350 degrees F before doing anything else and grease a 10-inch bundt pan.
2. In a bowl, mix together the cake mix, butterscotch pudding mix and vanilla pudding mix.
3. Add the eggs, oil and water and mix till well combined.
4. In another bowl, mix together the brown sugar, cinnamon and walnuts.
5. Place half of the cake mix mixture into the pan evenly and top with the half of the walnut mixture.
6. Now, place the remaining cake mix mixture and top with the remaining walnut mixture.
7. Cook in the oven for about 20 minutes.
8. Now, set the oven to 325 degrees F and cook the cake for about 35-40 minutes more.

STRAWBERRY
Punch Cake

Prep Time: 15 mins
Total Time: 1 hr 20 mins

Servings per Recipe: 12
Calories   290 kcal
Fat   5 g
Carbohydrates   58.3g
Protein   3.1 g
Cholesterol   1 mg
Sodium   331 mg

Ingredients

2 C. crushed fresh strawberries
1 (6 oz.) package strawberry flavored Jell-O(R) mix
3 C. miniature marshmallows
1 (18 oz.) package yellow cake mix, batter prepared as directed on package

Directions

1. Set your oven to 350 degrees F before doing anything else.
2. In the bottom of a 13x9-inch baking dish, spread the crushed strawberries and sprinkle with the dry gelatin powder and then top with the mini marshmallows.
3. Mix the cake mix according to the package's directions.
4. Transfer the mixture into the pan over the marshmallows and cook in the oven for about 40-50 minutes or till a toothpick inserted in the center comes out clean.

Gift Cake

🥣 Prep Time: 30 mins
🕐 Total Time: 1 hr 45 mins

Servings per Recipe: 24
Calories   251 kcal
Fat   12.3 g
Carbohydrates   33.6 g
Protein   2.4 g
Cholesterol   36 mg
Sodium   161 mg

Ingredients

- 1 (18.25 oz.) package yellow cake mix
- 3/4 C. vegetable oil
- 4 eggs
- 1 (8 oz.) container sour cream
- 1 C. brown sugar
- 1 tbsp ground cinnamon
- 2 C. confectioners' sugar
- 4 tbsp milk
- 1 tbsp vanilla extract

Directions

1. Set your oven to 325 degrees F before doing anything else.
2. In a large bowl, add the cake mix, sour cream, eggs and oil and beat till most the large lumps are gone.
3. Transfer half of the mixture into an ungreased 13x9-inch glass baking dish evenly.
4. In a small bowl, mix together the brown sugar and cinnamon and sprinkle over the cake mixture evenly.
5. Top with the remaining cake mix evenly and with a knife, twirl the cake till it looks like a honey bun.
6. Cook in the oven for about 40 minutes or till a toothpick inserted in the center comes out clean.
7. Meanwhile for frosting in a small bowl, add the confectioner's sugar, milk and vanilla and beat till smooth.
8. Spread the frosting over hot cake and serve warm.

CHOCOLATE
Coffee Cake

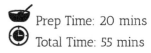
Prep Time: 20 mins
Total Time: 55 mins

Servings per Recipe: 12
Calories 320 kcal
Fat 11.3 g
Carbohydrates 53.2g
Protein 4.9 g
Cholesterol 33 mg
Sodium 359 mg

Ingredients

- 2 C. all-purpose flour
- 2 C. white sugar
- 3/4 C. unsweetened cocoa
- 2 tsp baking soda
- 1 tsp baking powder
- 1/2 tsp salt
- 2 eggs
- 1 C. cold brewed coffee
- 1 C. milk
- 1/2 C. vegetable oil
- 2 tsp vinegar

Directions

1. Set your oven to 350 degrees F before doing anything else and grease and flour a 13x9-inch cake pan.
2. In a large bowl, mix together the flour, cocoa powder, sugar, baking powder, baking soda and salt.
3. Make a well in the center of the mixture.
4. Add the eggs, coffee, milk, oil and vinegar and mix till smooth.
5. Transfer the mixture into the prepared pan and cook in the oven for about 35-40 minutes or till a toothpick inserted in the center comes out clean.

German Style Chocolate Cake

🥣 Prep Time: 40 mins
🕐 Total Time: 1 hr 10 mins

Servings per Recipe: 24
Calories   430 kcal
Fat   25.4 g
Carbohydrates   48.1g
Protein   5.2 g
Cholesterol   109 mg
Sodium   239 mg

Ingredients

4 (1 oz.) squares German sweet chocolate
1/2 C. water
2 C. all-purpose flour
1 tsp baking soda
1/4 tsp salt
1 C. butter, softened
2 C. white sugar
4 egg yolks
1 tsp vanilla extract
1 C. buttermilk
4 egg whites
12 fluid oz. evaporated milk

1 1/2 C. white sugar
3/4 C. butter
4 egg yolks
1 1/2 tsp vanilla extract
1 (8 oz.) package flaked coconut
1 1/2 C. chopped pecans

Directions

1. Set your oven to 350 degrees F before doing anything else and line a 13x9-inch pan with the parchment paper.
2. In a microwave safe bowl, add the chocolate and water and microwave on high for about 1 1/2 to 2 minutes, stirring once in the middle way.
3. In a medium bowl, mix together the flour, baking soda and salt.
4. In another large bowl, add 1 C. of the butter and 2 C. of the sugar and beat till fluffy and light.
5. Add 4 egg yolks one at a time, beating continuously.
6. Stir in the chocolate and 1 tsp of the vanilla extract.
7. Slowly, add the flour mixture alternately with the buttermilk, beating continuously till smooth.
8. In a third bowl, add the egg whites and beat on high till the soft peaks form.

9. Gently fold into the flour mixture.
10. Transfer the mixture into the prepared pan and cook in the oven for about 30 minutes or till a toothpick inserted in the center comes out clean.
11. For frosting in a large pan, mix together the milk, 1 1/2 C. of the sugar, 3/4 C. of the butter, 4 egg yolks and 1 1/2 tsp of the vanilla on medium heat and cook, stirring for about 12 minutes.
12. Remove from the heat and stir in the coconut and pecans.
13. Keep aside in the room temperature to cool.

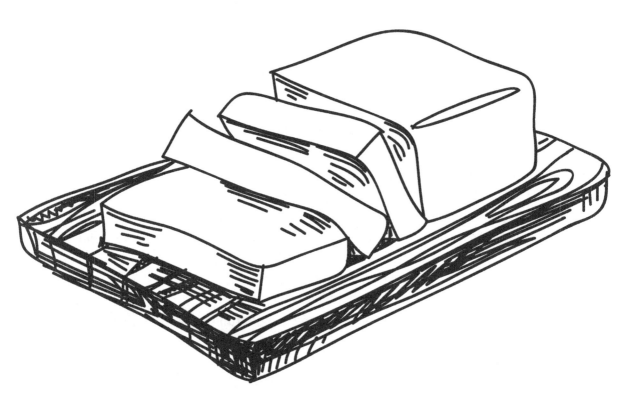

Buttermilk Chocolate Cake

Prep Time: 40 mins
Total Time: 1 hr

Servings per Recipe: 14
Calories   684 kcal
Fat   35.4 g
Carbohydrates   87.1g
Protein   11.6 g
Cholesterol   80 mg
Sodium   393 mg

Ingredients

- 2 C. all-purpose flour
- 2 C. white sugar
- 1 tsp baking soda
- 1 C. butter
- 1/2 C. unsweetened cocoa powder
- 1 C. buttermilk
- 2 eggs, beaten
- 1 tsp vanilla extract

- 1 1/2 C. creamy peanut butter
- 1/2 C. butter
- 1/4 C. unsweetened cocoa powder
- 1/3 C. buttermilk
- 4 C. sifted confectioners' sugar
- 1 tsp vanilla extract

Directions

1. Set your oven to 350 degrees F before doing anything else and grease and flour a 13x9-inch baking pan.
2. In a large bowl, mix together flour, white sugar and baking soda.
3. In a heavy pan, melt 1 C. of the butter on medium heat and stir in 1/2 C. of the cocoa powder. Add the buttermilk and eggs and stir till well combined.
4. Bring to a boil, stirring continuously. Remove from the heat and stir in the flour mixture, stirring till smooth. Stir in 1 tsp of the vanilla.
5. Transfer the mixture into the prepared baking pan and cook in the oven for about 20-25 minutes or till a toothpick inserted in the center comes out clean.
6. Cool for about 10 minutes on a wire rack.
7. Carefully spread peanut butter over warm cake and let it cool completely.
8. For frosting in a small pan, mix together 1/2 C. of the butter, 1/4 C. of the cocoa powder and buttermilk on medium heat and bring to a boil, stirring continuously.
9. Place the mixture over the confectioners' sugar, stirring till smooth.
10. Stir in 1 tsp of the vanilla.
11. Spread chocolate frosting over peanut butter on cake.

SEMI-SWEET
Chocolate Cake

Prep Time: 15 mins
Total Time: 1 hr 55 mins

Servings per Recipe: 8
Calories   285 kcal
Fat   18.6 g
Carbohydrates   29.9g
Protein   4.5 g
Cholesterol   100 mg
Sodium   109 mg

Ingredients

4 (1 oz.) squares semisweet chocolate, chopped
1/2 C. butter
3/4 C. white sugar
1/2 C. cocoa powder

3 eggs, beaten
1 tsp vanilla extract

Directions

1. Set your oven to 300 degrees F before doing anything else and grease an 8-inch round cake pan and dust with the cocoa powder.
2. In the top of a double boiler over lightly simmering water, melt the chocolate and butter.
3. Remove from the heat and stir in the sugar, cocoa powder, eggs and vanilla.
4. Transfer the mixture into the prepared pan and cook in the oven for about 30 minutes.
5. Let the cake cool in the pan for about 10 minutes, then turn out onto a wire rack and cool completely.

Cookout Cake

Prep Time: 15 mins
Total Time: 1 hr

Servings per Recipe: 24
Calories	155 kcal
Fat	5.5 g
Carbohydrates	25.7g
Protein	2.3 g
Cholesterol	16 mg
Sodium	240 mg

Ingredients

- 1 3/4 C. all-purpose flour
- 2 C. white sugar
- 3/4 C. unsweetened cocoa powder
- 2 tsp baking soda
- 1 tsp baking powder
- 1 tsp salt
- 2 eggs
- 1 C. strong brewed coffee
- 1 C. buttermilk
- 1/2 C. vegetable oil
- 1 tsp vanilla extract

Directions

1. Set your oven to 350 degrees F before doing anything else and grease 2 (9-inch) cake pans.
2. In large bowl mix together the flour, sugar, cocoa powder, baking soda, baking powder and salt.
3. Make a well in the center of the mixture.
4. Add the eggs, coffee, buttermilk, oil and vanilla and with an electric mixer, beat for 2 minutes on medium speed.
5. Transfer the mixture into the prepared pans and cook in the oven for about 30-40 minutes or till a toothpick inserted in the center comes out clean.
6. Remove from pans and finish cooling on a wire rack.
7. Fill and frost as desired.

OCTOBER'S
Cake

Prep Time: 15 mins
Total Time: 1 hr 10 mins

Servings per Recipe: 12
Calories	229 kcal
Fat	8.5 g
Carbohydrates	36.8g
Protein	5.2 g
Cholesterol	62 mg
Sodium	180 mg

Ingredients

1 1/2 C. semisweet chocolate chips
1 (19 oz.) can garbanzo beans, rinsed and drained
4 eggs
3/4 C. white sugar
1/2 tsp baking powder
1 tbsp confectioners' sugar for dusting

Directions

1. Set your oven to 350 degrees F before doing anything else and grease a 9-inch round cake pan.
2. In a microwave safe bowl, place the chocolate chips and microwave on high for about 2 minutes, stirring after every 20 seconds.
3. In a food processor, add the beans and eggs and pulse till smooth.
4. Add the sugar and the baking powder and pulse to combine.
5. Add the melted chocolate and pulse till smooth, scraping down the corners to make sure chocolate is completely mixed.
6. Transfer the mixture into the prepared pan and cook in the oven for about 40 minutes or till a toothpick inserted in the center comes out clean.
7. Cool in the pan on a wire rack for about 10-15 minutes before inverting onto a serving plate.
8. Dust with confectioners' sugar just before serving.

Alabama Inspired Cake

Prep Time: 15 mins
Total Time: 55 mins

Servings per Recipe: 12
Calories   513 kcal
Fat   25.7 g
Carbohydrates   66.6 g
Protein   5.8 g
Cholesterol   74 mg
Sodium   502 mg

Ingredients

- 2 tbsp unsweetened cocoa powder
- 2 oz. red food coloring
- 1 C. buttermilk
- 1 tsp salt
- 1 tsp vanilla extract
- 1/2 C. shortening
- 1 1/2 C. white sugar
- 2 eggs
- 2 1/2 C. all-purpose flour, sifted
- 1 1/2 tsp baking soda
- 1 tsp white vinegar
- 1 C. milk
- 5 tbsp all-purpose flour
- 1 C. white sugar
- 1 C. butter
- 1 tsp vanilla extract

Directions

1. Set your oven to 350 degrees F before doing anything else and grease 2 (9-inch) round cake pan.
2. In a small bowl, mix together the cocoa powder and food coloring.
3. In a bowl, add the buttermilk, salt and 1 tsp of the vanilla and mix well.
4. In another large bowl, add the shortening and 1 1/2 C. of the sugar and beat till fluffy and light.
5. Add the eggs, one at a time, beating continuously, then stir in the cocoa mixture.
6. Add the buttermilk mixture alternately with the flour, mixing till just combined.
7. Mix together the baking soda and vinegar and then gently fold into the cake mixture.
8. Transfer the mixture into the prepared pans and cook in the oven for about 30 minutes or till a toothpick inserted in the center comes out clean.
9. Allow to cool completely before frosting. Refrigerate until ready to serve.
10. For icing in a pan, mix together the milk and 5 tbsp flour on low heat and cook, stirring continuously till the mixture becomes thick.
11. Keep aside to cool completely.

12. In a bowl, add the butter, 1 C. of the sugar and 1 tsp of the vanilla and beat till fluffy and light.
13. Stir in the cooled milk and flour mixture, beating until icing reaches spreading consistency.

Cinnamon Fudgy Cake

Prep Time: 15 mins
Total Time: 1 hr 5 mins

Servings per Recipe: 24
Calories	269 kcal
Fat	17.5 g
Carbohydrates	27.2g
Protein	3.4 g
Cholesterol	31 mg
Sodium	188 mg

Ingredients

- 2 C. all-purpose flour
- 2 C. white sugar
- 3/4 C. unsweetened cocoa powder
- 2 tsp baking soda
- 1 tsp baking powder
- 1/2 tsp salt
- 1 tsp ground cinnamon
- 4 eggs
- 1 1/2 C. vegetable oil
- 3 C. grated zucchini
- 3/4 C. chopped walnuts

Directions

1. Set your oven to 350 degrees F before doing anything else and grease a 13x9-inch round baking pan.
2. In a medium bowl, mix together the flour, sugar, cocoa powder, baking soda, baking powder, salt and cinnamon.
3. Add the eggs and oil and mix well.
4. Fold in the zucchini and walnuts.
5. Transfer the mixture into the prepared pan and cook in the oven for about 50-60 minutes or till a toothpick inserted in the center comes out clean.

CHEESECAKE
Japanese Style

🥣 Prep Time: 35 mins
🕐 Total Time: 1 hr 20 mins

Servings per Recipe: 8
Calories 99 kcal
Fat 5 g
Carbohydrates 10.8g
Protein 2.9 g
Cholesterol 64 mg
Sodium 51 mg

Ingredients

1 (3 oz.) package cream cheese
1/4 C. milk
2 egg yolks
1/4 C. white sugar, divided
2 egg whites
1/3 tsp cream of tartar
3 tbsp all-purpose flour
1 1/2 tbsp cornstarch

Directions

1. Set your oven to 350 degrees F before doing anything else and line a 9-inch round cake pan with the parchment paper.
2. In a small pan, add the cream cheese and milk on medium-low heat and cook, stirring occasionally till the cream cheese melts. Remove from the heat and keep aside.
3. In a medium bowl, add the egg yolks and half of the sugar and with an electric mixer, beat till fluffy and light. Fold the cream cheese mixture into the yolks.
4. Sift in the flour and cornstarch and stir till well combined.
5. In another bowl, add the egg whites and cream of tartar and beat till soft peaks form.
6. Slowly, add the remaining sugar and continue beating till the stiff peaks form.
7. Fold the egg whites into the cream cheese mixture.
8. Place the mixture into the prepared cake pan.
9. Arrange the cake pan onto a baking dish and pour water into the baking dish to half way full. Cook in the oven for about 20 minutes.
10. Now, set the oven to 300 degrees F and cook for about 15 minutes more.
11. Let the cake cool before removing from the pan.
12. Run a knife around the outer edge of the cake pan, and invert onto a plate to remove the cake.
13. Peel off the parchment paper and invert onto a serving plate so the top of the cake is on top again.

Maple Pecan Cheesecake

Prep Time: 40 mins
Total Time: 1 hr 20 mins

Servings per Recipe: 12
Calories 450 kcal
Fat 30.6 g
Carbohydrates 39.2g
Protein 6.6 g
Cholesterol 112 mg
Sodium 224 mg

Ingredients

- 1/4 C. butter
- 1 C. graham cracker crumbs
- 3 tbsp packed brown sugar
- 1/3 C. chopped pecans
- 2 (8 oz.) packages cream cheese, softened
- 1 1/4 C. packed brown sugar
- 3 eggs
- 1 tsp vanilla extract
- 1/4 C. sour cream
- 1/3 C. chopped pecans
- 1 1/2 C. sour cream
- 1/4 C. packed brown sugar
- 3/4 tsp maple flavored extract

Directions

1. Set your oven to 350 degrees F before doing anything else.
2. For the crust in a small pan, melt the butter.
3. Stir in the graham cracker crumbs, 3 tbsp of the brown sugar and 1/3 C. of the walnuts.
4. Place the mixture into a 9-inch into ungreased spring form pan.
5. For filling in a bowl, add the cream cheese and 1 1/4 C. of the brown sugar and beat till smooth and fluffy. Slowly add the eggs, one at a time, beating till just combined.
6. Stir in 1 tsp of the vanilla, 1/4 C. of the sour cream and 1/3 C. of the walnuts.
7. Place the filling over the crust and cook in the oven for about 55-60 minutes.
8. Place the pan onto the rack.
9. Meanwhile for the topping in a bowl, mix together 1 1/2 C. of the sour cream, 1/4 C. of the brown sugar, maple flavoring and 1/2 tsp of the remaining flavoring.
10. Spread the mixture over the cheesecake.
11. Cook in the oven for about 10 minutes more.
12. Loosen the sides of the cake and cool at almost room temperature.
13. Refrigerate to chill for a few hours before serving.

DELIGHTFUL Cheesecake

Prep Time: 20 mins
Total Time: 1 hr 30 mins

Servings per Recipe: 12
Calories 324 kcal
Fat 21.2 g
Carbohydrates 28.1g
Protein 5.1 g
Cholesterol 80 mg
Sodium 200 mg

Ingredients

- 1 (9 inch) prepared shortbread pie crust
- 2 (8 oz.) packages cream cheese
- 1 C. white sugar
- 2 eggs
- 2 tsp vanilla extract
- 1 C. sour cream

Directions

1. Set your oven to 325 degrees F before doing anything else.
2. In a bowl, add the cream cheese and sugar and beat well.
3. Add the eggs one at time, beating till well combined.
4. Add the vanilla and sour cream and mix, then transfer into the shortbread crust.
5. Cook in the oven for about 60-70 minutes
6. Run a knife around the outside edge, but leave the cake in the pan.
7. Let it cool on the counter, then place in refrigerator.
8. Remove from pan when completely chilled, and serve.

Expresso Cheesecake

Prep Time: 35 mins
Total Time: 10 hrs 3 mins

Servings per Recipe: 12
Calories	486 kcal
Fat	35 g
Carbohydrates	37.1 g
Protein	7.7 g
Cholesterol	141 mg
Sodium	363 mg

Ingredients

- 2 C. graham cracker crumbs
- 1/2 C. butter, melted
- 2 tbsp white sugar
- 3 (8 oz.) packages cream cheese, softened
- 1 C. white sugar
- 3 eggs
- 1 (8 oz.) container sour cream
- 1/4 C. brewed espresso or strong coffee
- 2 tsp vanilla extract
- pressurized whipped cream
- caramel ice cream topping

Directions

1. Set your oven to 350 degrees F before doing anything else and grease a 9-inch spring form pan.
2. In a bowl, mix together the graham cracker crumbs, melted butter and 2 tbsp of the sugar.
3. Place the mixture into the bottom and 1-inch up the sides of an 8 inch spring form pan and press to smooth. Cook in the oven for about 8 minutes.
4. Now, set the oven to 325 degrees F.
5. In a large bowl, add the softened cream cheese and with an electric mixer and beat till fluffy. Slowly, add 1 C. of the sugar, beating till well combined.
6. Add eggs, one at a time, beating well.
7. Stir in the sour cream, espresso and vanilla.
8. Transfer the mixture into the prepared pan and cook in the oven for about 65 minutes.
9. Turn the oven off, partially open the door and allow the cheesecake to rest for about 15 minutes more. Remove from the oven, and run a knife around the edges.
10. Cool the cheesecake on a wire rack at room temperature.
11. Cover the spring form pan with a plastic wrap, and refrigerate to chill for about 8 hours.
12. To serve, cut the cheesecake into wedges and garnish each slice with whipped cream and caramel sauce.

EAST COAST STYLE
Cheesecake

Prep Time: 30 mins
Total Time: 1 hr 30 mins

Servings per Recipe: 12
Calories   371 kcal
Fat   26.7 g
Carbohydrates   27.7g
Protein   6.8 g
Cholesterol   117 mg
Sodium   232 mg

Ingredients

1 1/2 C. finely ground graham cracker crumbs
2 tbsp white sugar
1/4 C. unsalted butter, melted
1 1/4 lb. cream cheese, softened
3/4 C. white sugar
1 C. sour cream
3 tbsp all-purpose flour
3 eggs
3/4 C. key lime juice
1 tsp vanilla extract

Directions

1. Set your oven to 375 degrees F before doing anything else.
2. For crust in a bowl mix together the graham cracker crumbs and 2 tbsp of the sugar.
3. Add the butter and stir till well combined.
4. Place the mixture into the bottom and 1 3/4-inch up the sides of an 8 inch spring form pan and press to smooth.
5. Cook in the oven for about 8 minutes.
6. Transfer the pan to a rack and cool.
7. In a large add the cream cheese and 3/4 C. sugar and with an electric mixer, beat till smooth.
8. Add the eggs, one at a time, beating well.
9. Add the sour cream, flour, lime juice and vanilla and beat till smooth.
10. Place the filling over the crust and cook in the oven for about 15 minutes.
11. Now, set the oven to 250 degrees F and cook for about 50-55 minutes more.
12. Let the cheesecake cool on a rack, then refrigerate, covered to chill for overnight.
13. Remove the cheesecake from the pan and transfer it to a cake stand.

Spanish Berry Cheesecake

Prep Time: 30 mins
Total Time: 1 hr 30 mins

Servings per Recipe: 10
Calories   490 kcal
Fat   30 g
Carbohydrates   41.4g
Protein   10 g
Cholesterol   127 mg
Sodium   368 mg

Ingredients

40 vanilla wafers, crushed
6 tbsp butter, melted
2 (8 oz.) packages cream cheese, softened
3/4 C. white sugar
2 tbsp all-purpose flour
2 tsp vanilla extract
1 C. cottage cheese, creamed
1/4 C. cherry brandy

3 eggs
3 1/2 C. fresh blackberries
1 tbsp cherry brandy
1 tbsp white sugar

Directions

1. Set your oven to 375 degrees F before doing anything else.
2. In a medium bowl, mix together the vanilla wafer crumbs and butter.
3. Place the mixture into the bottom and 1 3/4-inch up the sides of an 8 inch spring form pan and press to smooth.
4. In another large bowl, add the cream cheese, 3/4 C. of the sugar, flour and vanilla and with an electric mixer, beat on low speed till smooth.
5. In a blender, place the cottage cheese and pulse till smooth.
6. Add the cottage cheese and 1/4 C. of the cherry brandy into the cream cheese mixture and mix well.
7. Add the eggs and beat on low speed till just combined.
8. Place half of the cheese mixture into the crust-lined pan.
9. Spread 1 C. of the blackberries on top.
10. Repeat the layers once
11. Arrange the spring form pan in a shallow baking pan and cook in the oven for about 40-45 minutes.
12. Cool on a wire rack for about 15 minutes.

13. Loosen the sides and cool completely on wire rack.
14. Refrigerate, covered to chill for at least 4 hours or until ready to serve.
15. For topping, in a medium bowl mix together the remaining 2 C. of the blackberries, 1 tbsp of the cherry brandy, and 1 tbsp of the sugar.
16. Cover the mixture and refrigerate to chill for up to 2 hours.
17. While serving, cut the cheesecake into wedges and top each serving with fruit topping.

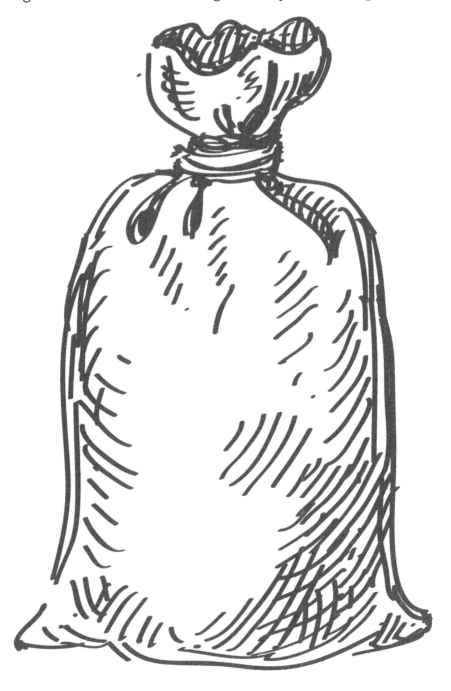

Potluck Cake

🥣 Prep Time: 30 mins
🕐 Total Time: 2 hrs

Servings per Recipe: 20
Calories   362 kcal
Fat   20.4 g
Carbohydrates   42.9 g
Protein   4.1 g
Cholesterol   50 mg
Sodium   283 mg

Ingredients

- 1 (15 oz.) can canned pumpkin puree
- 2 C. white sugar
- 1 C. vegetable oil
- 4 eggs
- 2 C. all-purpose flour
- 2 tsp baking soda
- 1 tsp ground cinnamon
- 1/2 tsp salt
- 1 (3 oz.) package cream cheese
- 5 tbsp butter, softened
- 1 tsp vanilla extract
- 1 3/4 C. confectioners' sugar
- 3 tsp milk
- 1 C. chopped walnuts

Directions

1. Set your oven to 350 degrees F before doing anything else and grease and flour a 15x10-inch baking pan.
2. In a bowl, add the pumpkin, 2 C. of the white sugar and oil and beat well.
3. Add the eggs and mix well.
4. In another bowl, mix together the flour, baking soda, cinnamon and salt.
5. Add the flour mixture into the pumpkin mixture and beat till well combined.
6. Transfer the mixture into the prepared pan and cook in the oven for about 25-30 minutes or till a toothpick inserted in the center comes out clean.
7. Let the cake cool.
8. In a mixing bowl, add the cream cheese, butter and vanilla and beat till smooth.
9. Slowly, add 1 3/4 C. of the confectioners' sugar and mix well.
10. Add the milk and mix till the frosting reaches desired spreading consistency.
11. Frost the cake and sprinkle with the walnuts.

CLASSIC
Cake

🥣 Prep Time: 15 mins
⏲ Total Time: 2 hrs 20 mins

Servings per Recipe: 16
Calories 617 kcal
Fat 30.3 g
Carbohydrates 75.5g
Protein 13.1 g
Cholesterol 61 mg
Sodium 198 mg

Ingredients

4 eggs
2 C. white sugar
1 tsp vanilla extract
2 C. all-purpose flour
1 tsp baking powder
1 C. milk
2 tbsp margarine

1 1/4 C. peanut butter
2 lb. milk chocolate candy bar, chopped

Directions

1. Set your oven to 350 degrees F before doing anything else and grease and flour a 15x10-inch baking pan.
2. In a bowl, sift together the flour and baking powder.
3. In another large bowl, add the eggs, sugar and vanilla and with an electric mixer, beat on high speed till light and lemon-colored.
4. Add the flour mixture and mix till well combined.
5. Microwave the milk and margarine for about 2 minutes.
6. Add the milk mixture into the flour mixture and mix till well combined.
7. Transfer the mixture into the prepared pan and cook in the oven for about 20-25 minutes or till a toothpick inserted in the center comes out clean.
8. When cake is cool, spread the peanut butter all over the cake.
9. Refrigerate for about 1 hour.
10. In a microwave safe dish, melt the chocolate and spread evenly over peanut butter layer.
11. Refrigerate till the chocolate becomes harden.

Super Moist Carrot Cake

🥣 Prep Time: 30 mins
🕐 Total Time: 2 hrs

Servings per Recipe: 18
Calories 575 kcal
Fat 34.8 g
Carbohydrates 63.7 g
Protein 5.1 g
Cholesterol 69 mg
Sodium 347 mg

Ingredients

- 4 eggs
- 1 1/4 C. vegetable oil
- 2 C. white sugar
- 2 tsp vanilla extract
- 2 C. all-purpose flour
- 2 tsp baking soda
- 2 tsp baking powder
- 1/2 tsp salt
- 2 tsp ground cinnamon
- 3 C. grated carrots
- 1 C. chopped pecans
- 1/2 C. butter, softened
- 8 oz. cream cheese, softened
- 4 C. confectioners' sugar
- 1 tsp vanilla extract
- 1 C. chopped pecans

Directions

1. Set your oven to 350 degrees F before doing anything else and grease and flour a 13x9-inch baking pan.
2. In a large bowl, add the eggs, oil, white sugar and 2 tsp of the vanilla and beat well.
3. Add the flour, baking soda, baking powder, salt and cinnamon and mix till well combined.
4. Fold in the carrots and pecans.
5. Transfer the mixture into the prepared pan and cook in the oven for about 40-50 minutes or till a toothpick inserted in the center comes out clean.
6. Let cool in pan for 10 minutes, then turn out onto a wire rack and cool completely.
7. For frosting in a medium bowl, add the butter, cream cheese, confectioners' sugar and 1 tsp of the vanilla and beat till the mixture is smooth and creamy.
8. Stir in chopped pecans.
9. Frost the cooled cake.

TRADITIONAL
Latin Cake

🥣 Prep Time: 40 mins
🕐 Total Time: 1 hr 40 mins

Servings per Recipe: 24
Calories	280 kcal
Fat	13.7 g
Carbohydrates	34.6g
Protein	5.5 g
Cholesterol	81 mg
Sodium	87 mg

Ingredients

1 1/2 C. all-purpose flour
1 tsp baking powder
1/2 C. unsalted butter
1 C. white sugar
5 eggs
1/2 tsp vanilla extract
2 C. whole milk

1 (14 oz.) can sweetened condensed milk
1 (12 fluid oz.) can evaporated milk
1 1/2 C. heavy whipping cream
1 C. white sugar
1 tsp vanilla extract

Directions

1. Set your oven to 350 degrees F before doing anything else and grease and flour a 13x9-inch baking pan.
2. In a bowl, sift together the flour and baking powder.
3. In another large bowl, add 1 C. of the sugar and butter and beat till fluffy.
4. Add eggs and 1/2 tsp of the vanilla extract and beat till well combined.
5. Slowly, add the flour mixture into sugar mixture, beating till just combine.
6. Transfer the mixture into the prepared pan and cook in the oven for about 30 minutes or till a toothpick inserted in the center comes out clean.
7. Remove from the oven and with a fork, pierce the cake several times.
8. In a bowl, mix together the whole milk, condensed milk and evaporated.
9. Place the milk mixture over the cooled cake.
10. In another bowl, add the whipping cream, remaining 1 C. of the sugar, and remaining 1 tsp of the vanilla and beat till thick.
11. Spread the cream mixture over the top of the cake.
12. Refrigerate before serving.

Surprisingly Crunchy Cake

Prep Time: 20 mins
Total Time: 1 hr

Servings per Recipe: 18
Calories   244 kcal
Fat   8.2 g
Carbohydrates   41.1g
Protein   2.5 g
Cholesterol   31 mg
Sodium   179 mg

Ingredients

- 1/2 C. butter
- 1 1/2 C. white sugar
- 1 egg
- 1 tsp vanilla extract
- 2 C. all-purpose flour
- 1 tsp baking soda
- 1/4 tsp salt
- 1 C. buttermilk
- 2 C. rhubarb, chopped
- 1 tbsp all-purpose flour
- 1/4 C. butter
- 2 tsp ground cinnamon
- 1 C. packed brown sugar

Directions

1. Set your oven to 350 degrees F before doing anything else and grease and flour a 13x9-inch baking pan.
2. In a bowl, sift together 2 C. of the flour, baking soda and salt.
3. In another large bowl, add the sugar and margarine and beat till fluffy and light.
4. Add egg and vanilla extract and beat till well combined.
5. Add the flour mixture alternately with the buttermilk, beating till just combine.
6. In a third bowl, add the rhubarb and 1 tbsp of the flour and toss to coat well.
7. Add the rhubarb mixture into the flour mixture and stir to combine.
8. Transfer the mixture into the prepared pan and cook in the oven for about 45 minutes or till a toothpick inserted in the center comes out clean.

COCOA Cake

🥣 Prep Time: 10 mins
🕐 Total Time: 50 mins

Servings per Recipe: 12
Calories   382 kcal
Fat   17.4 g
Carbohydrates   52.3g
Protein   6 g
Cholesterol   49 mg
Sodium   557 mg

Ingredients

- 1 C. margarine
- 1 3/4 C. white sugar
- 3 eggs
- 1 1/2 tsp vanilla extract
- 1 1/2 C. milk
- 2 1/2 C. all-purpose flour
- 6 tbsp unsweetened cocoa powder
- 1 1/2 tsp baking soda
- 1 tsp salt

Directions

1. Set your oven to 350 degrees F before doing anything else and grease and flour a 13x9-inch baking pan.
2. In a bowl, sift together the flour, cocoa powder, baking soda and salt.
3. In another large bowl, add the sugar and margarine and beat till fluffy and light.
4. Add eggs one at a time, beating continuously.
5. Stir in the vanilla extract.
6. Add the flour mixture alternately with the milk, beating till just combine.
7. Transfer the mixture into the prepared pan and cook in the oven for about 40-45 minutes or till a toothpick inserted in the center comes out clean.

Rustic Cake

Prep Time: 20 mins
Total Time: 1 hr

Servings per Recipe: 24
Calories   139 kcal
Fat   5.2 g
Carbohydrates   21.2g
Protein   2.2 g
Cholesterol   24 mg
Sodium   181 mg

Ingredients

- 2 C. all-purpose flour
- 1 1/2 C. white sugar
- 1/2 C. shortening
- 1 C. milk
- 3 1/2 tsp baking powder
- 1 tsp salt
- 1 tsp vanilla extract
- 3 eggs

Directions

1. Set your oven to 350 degrees F before doing anything else and grease and flour a 13x9-inch baking pan.
2. In a bowl, mix together the flour, baking powder and salt.
3. In another large bowl, add the sugar and shortening and beat till fluffy and light.
4. Add eggs one at a time, beating continuously.
5. Stir in the vanilla extract.
6. Add the flour mixture alternately with the milk, beating till just combine.
7. Transfer the mixture into the prepared pan and cook in the oven for about 40-45 minutes or till a toothpick inserted in the center comes out clean.

ARTISANAL STYLE
Cake

Prep Time: 20 mins
Total Time: 50 mins

Servings per Recipe: 12
Calories 208 kcal
Fat 8.9 g
Carbohydrates 29.5g
Protein 3.1 g
Cholesterol 52 mg
Sodium 143 mg

Ingredients

1/3 C. brown sugar
1 tsp ground cinnamon
2/3 C. white sugar
1/2 C. butter, softened
2 eggs
1 1/2 tsp vanilla extract
1 1/2 C. all-purpose flour

1 3/4 tsp baking powder
1/2 C. milk
1 apple, peeled and chopped

Directions

1. Set your oven to 350 degrees F before doing anything else and grease a 9x5-inch loaf pan.
2. In a bowl, mix together the brown sugar and cinnamon.
3. In another bowl, add the butter and white sugar and with an electric mixer, beat till smooth and creamy.
4. Add the eggs, 1 at a time, beating continuously till well combined, then stir in the vanilla extract.
5. In a bowl, mix together the flour and baking powder.
6. Add the milk into mixture and mix till smooth.
7. Place half of the mixture into the prepared loaf pan evenly.
8. Place half of the apples, followed by half the brown sugar mixture over the flour mixture.
9. Lightly pat apple mixture into mixture.
10. Repeat the layers once and lightly pat apples into the mixture.
11. With a spoon, swirl the brown sugar mixture through apples.
12. Cook in the oven for about 30-40 minutes or till a toothpick inserted in the center comes out clean.

Cinnamon Apple Cake

Prep Time: 20 mins
Total Time: 1 hr 5 mins

Servings per Recipe: 12
Calories	406 kcal
Fat	19.6 g
Carbohydrates	57 g
Protein	3.5 g
Cholesterol	31 mg
Sodium	288 mg

Ingredients

- 3 lb. apples - peeled, cored and sliced
- 2 C. all-purpose flour
- 1 1/2 C. white sugar
- 2 tsp baking powder
- 1 tsp salt
- 2 eggs, beaten
- 1 C. vegetable oil
- 1 tsp ground cinnamon

Directions

1. Set your oven to 350 degrees F before doing anything else and grease a 13x9-inch baking pan.
2. In the bottom of the prepared pan, arrange the apple slices.
3. In a bowl, mix together the flour, sugar, baking powder, and salt.
4. Add the eggs and oil and mix till well combined.
5. Place the mixture over the apples and sprinkle with the cinnamon.
6. Cook in the oven for about 40-45 minutes.

RAISINS and Walnuts Cake

Prep Time: 20 mins
Total Time: 40 mins

Servings per Recipe: 12
Calories   267 kcal
Fat   11.1 g
Carbohydrates   40.5g
Protein   3.2 g
Cholesterol   20 mg
Sodium   161 mg

Ingredients

1/2 C. butter
1 C. white sugar
1 C. chilled applesauce
2 C. all-purpose flour
1 tsp baking soda
1 tsp ground cinnamon
1/4 tsp ground cloves

1/2 C. raisins
1/2 C. chopped walnuts

Directions

1. Set your oven to 35 degrees F before doing anything else and grease and flour an 8-inch square pan.
2. In a bowl, add the butter and sugar and beat till creamy.
3. Transfer the mixture into the prepared pan and cook in the oven for about 40 minutes or till a toothpick inserted in the center comes out clean.

Lemony Lemon Cake

Prep Time: 30 mins
Total Time: 3 hrs

Servings per Recipe: 14
Calories   459 kcal
Fat   19.4 g
Carbohydrates   66.9 g
Protein   6.9 g
Cholesterol   173 mg
Sodium   344 mg

Ingredients

1 3/4 C. cake flour
1 tbsp baking powder
1 tsp salt
1/2 C. white sugar
1/2 C. vegetable oil
6 egg yolks
3/4 C. water
1 tbsp lemon zest

6 egg whites
1/2 tsp cream of tartar
3/4 C. white sugar
1 C. heavy whipping cream
2 1/2 C. lemon pie filling
8 slices lemon

Directions

1. Set your oven to 350 degrees F before doing anything else.
2. In a large bowl, mix together the flour, baking powder, salt, and 1/2 C. sugar.
3. Add the oil, egg yolks, water and lemon rind and beat with an electric mixer till smooth.
4. In a small bowl, add the egg whites and cream of tartar and beat till peaks form.
5. Slowly, add 3/4 C. of the sugar and beat till very stiff and shiny peaks form.
6. Fold 1/3 of the whites into the flour mixture, then quickly fold in the remaining whites.
7. Transfer the mixture into ungreased 10-inch tube pan and cook in the oven for about 60 minutes or till a toothpick inserted in the center comes out clean.
8. Let the cake cool completely in the pan.
9. When cool, loosen edges and shake pan to remove cake.
10. For filling in a bow, add cream and beat till stiff peaks form.
11. Fold in the lemon filling and refrigerate to chill till stiff.
12. To assemble the cake, slice the cake horizontally into 3 equal layers.
13. Fill layers with 1/3 C. of the filling.
14. Spread remaining filling on top layer. Decorate with lemon slices.

LOUISIANA
Cajun Cake

Prep Time: 1 hr
Total Time: 3 hrs

Servings per Recipe: 12
Calories   459 kcal
Fat   19.4 g
Carbohydrates   66.9g
Protein   6.9 g
Cholesterol   173 mg
Sodium   344 mg

Ingredients

Cake:
4 eggs, separated
3 1/2 C. sifted cake flour
1 tbsp baking powder
3/4 C. butter, room temperature
2 C. white sugar
1/2 tsp salt
1 C. milk, room temperature
1 tsp lemon juice
1 tsp vanilla extract
Custard:
2 C. white sugar, divided
1/2 tsp salt
1/4 C. all-purpose flour
1/4 C. cornstarch
1/4 C. unsweetened cocoa powder
2 (1 oz.) squares bittersweet chocolate, chopped

4 large eggs, beaten
4 C. whole milk
1 tbsp butter, room temperature
1 tbsp vanilla extract
Buttercream Frosting:
1 C. butter, softened
3 C. confectioners' sugar, sifted
1 C. unsweetened cocoa powder, sifted
1 tsp vanilla extract
1 tbsp hot water (optional)
Ganache:
2 C. semisweet chocolate chips
2 C. heavy whipping cream
2 tsp vanilla extract

Directions

1. Set your oven to 375 degrees F before doing anything else and grease a 3 (9-inch) cake pans.
2. In a glass bowl, add the 4 egg whites and beat till the stiff peaks form.
3. Lift your beater straight up, the tip of the peak formed by the egg whites should curl over slightly.
4. In another bowl, sift together the cake flour and baking powder.
5. In a third bowl, add 3/4 C. of the butter, 2 C. of the sugar, and 1/2 tsp of the salt and with

an electric mixer, beat till fluffy and light.
6. Add the egg yolks, one at a time, beating continuously.
7. Add the cake flour mixture alternately with 1 C. of the milk, mixing till well combined.
8. Stir in the lemon juice and 1 tsp of the vanilla extract.
9. With a rubber spatula, fold about 1/3 of the egg whites mixture into the flour mixture to lighten it.
10. Fold in the remaining egg whites, mixing till just combined.
11. Transfer the mixture into the prepared pans and cook in the oven for about 15-20 minutes or till a toothpick inserted in the center comes out clean.
12. Cool in pans for 5 minutes, then invert onto cooling racks to cool completely.
13. For custard in a pan, mix together the flour, cornstarch, 1/4 C. of the cocoa powder, 1 1/2 C. of the sugar and 1/2 tsp of the salt.
14. In a bowl, add the remaining 1/2 C. of the sugar and 4 beaten eggs and beat well.
15. Place 4 C. of the whole milk into pan on medium heat and bring to a boil, stirring continuously.
16. Remove from the heat and slowly pour hot milk mixture into the egg mixture, beating continuously.
17. Add the chopped chocolate and stir till the chocolate is melted.
18. Return custard to the pan on medium heat and cook, stirring continuously for about 5 minutes.
19. Remove from the heat and stir in 1 tbsp of the butter and 1 tbsp of the vanilla extract.
20. Transfer the custard into a bowl and keep aside to cool.
21. For the butter cream in a bowl, place 1 C. of the softened butter and slowly, beat in 3 C. of the sifted confectioners' sugar.
22. Add 1 C. of the sifted cocoa powder and 1 tsp of the vanilla extract and beat till smooth.
23. (Add a tbsp of hot water or as needed.)
24. For ganache in a large bowl, place the chocolate chips.
25. In a pan, heat the heavy cream till very hot but not boiling.
26. Remove from the heat and immediately, place over the chocolate chips and keep aside for about 3 minutes.
27. Beat the chocolate mixture by scraping the sides and bottom of the bowl till smooth.
28. Stir in 2 tsp of the vanilla extract and keep aside to cool. (Ganache should be spreadable and not fir.)
29. For assembling the cake with a long knife and a gentle sawing motion, slice each cake layer in half horizontally.
30. Cover the cake plate with the strips of parchment paper.
31. Put a dab of butter cream in the center of the plate to keep cake from shifting.
32. Place a cake half on the plate and spread custard filling onto cake layer, leaving the edges.

33. Gently, place another cake round on top of the first and repeat with another custard layer.
34. Repeat with the remaining layers and custard, topping custard with the last cake layer.
35. Refrigerate the cake to chill for about 30 minutes.
36. Frost top and sides of cake with the chocolate butter cream and refrigerate to chill for about 30 minutes.
37. Top the frosted cake with the ganache.
38. Remove the parchment strips from the cake plate.

Chocolate Cheesecake Irish Style

Prep Time: 20 mins
Total Time: 9 hrs 20 mins

Servings per Recipe: 12
Calories 457 kcal
Fat 29.2 g
Carbohydrates 42.4g
Protein 8.1 g
Cholesterol 123 mg
Sodium 298 mg

Ingredients

- 1 1/2 C. chocolate cookie crumbs
- 1/3 C. confectioners' sugar
- 1/3 C. unsweetened cocoa powder
- 1/4 C. butter
- 3 (8 oz.) packages cream cheese, softened
- 1 1/4 C. white sugar
- 1/4 C. unsweetened cocoa powder
- 3 tbsp all-purpose flour
- 3 eggs
- 1/2 C. sour cream
- 1/4 C. Irish cream liqueur

Directions

1. Set your oven to 350 degrees F before doing anything else.
2. In a large bowl, mix together the cookie crumbs, confectioners' sugar and 1/3 C. of the cocoa powder.
3. Add the melted butter and mix till well combined.
4. Place the mixture into the bottom of a 9 inch spring form pan and press to smooth.
5. Cook in the oven for about 10 minutes then remove from the oven and keep aside.
6. Now, set the oven to 450 degrees F.
7. In a large bowl, add the cream cheese, flour, white sugar and 1/4 C. of the cocoa powder and beat at medium speed till smooth.
8. Add eggs, one at a time, beating continuously.
9. Add the sour cream and Irish cream liqueur, mixing on low speed.
10. Transfer the filling mixture over the baked crust evenly.
11. Cook in the oven for about 10 minutes.
12. Now, set the oven to 250 degrees F and cook for about 60 minutes.
13. With a knife, loosen the cake from rim of the pan and let it cool.
14. Remove the rim of the pan and refrigerate to chill before serving

NOVEMBER'S
Cheesecakes

Prep Time: 30 mins
Total Time: 4 hrs 10 mins

Servings per Recipe: 8
Calories	426 kcal
Fat	29 g
Carbohydrates	35.5g
Protein	7.2 g
Cholesterol	108 mg
Sodium	354 mg

Ingredients

- 2 (8 oz.) packages cream cheese, softened
- 1/2 C. white sugar
- 1/2 tsp vanilla extract
- 2 eggs
- 1 (9 inch) prepared graham cracker crust
- 1/2 C. pumpkin puree
- 1/2 tsp ground cinnamon
- 1 pinch ground cloves
- 1 pinch ground nutmeg
- 1/2 C. frozen whipped topping, thawed

Directions

1. Set your oven to 325 degrees F before doing anything else.
2. In a large bowl, add the cream cheese, sugar and vanilla and beat till smooth.
3. Add the eggs, one at a time, beating continuously.
4. Transfer 1 C. of the mixture into the bottom of the crust evenly.
5. In the remaining mixture, add the pumpkin, cinnamon, cloves and nutmeg and stir gently till well combined.
6. Carefully, spread over the mixture in the crust and cook in the oven for about 35-40 minutes.
7. Let it cool, then refrigerate for about 3 hours or overnight.
8. Cover with the whipped topping before serving.

Party-Time Cheesecakes

Prep Time: 30 mins
Total Time: 45 mins

Servings per Recipe: 48
Calories   95 kcal
Fat   4.8 g
Carbohydrates   11.8g
Protein   1.3 g
Cholesterol   18 mg
Sodium   54 mg

Ingredients

1 (12 oz.) package vanilla wafers, crushed
2 (8 oz.) packages cream cheese
3/4 C. white sugar
2 eggs
1 tsp vanilla extract
1 (21 oz.) can cherry pie filling

Directions

1. Set your oven to 350 degrees F before doing anything else and line miniature muffin tins with miniature paper liners.
2. Pace about 1/2 tsp of the crushed vanilla wafers into each paper cup.
3. In a bowl, add the cream cheese, sugar, eggs and vanilla and beat till fluffy and light.
4. Fill each miniature muffin liner with the cream cheese mixture, almost to the top.
5. Cook in the oven for about 15 minutes.
6. Top with a tsp of the cherry pie filling and serve.

MOVIE TIME
Cake

🥣 Prep Time: 20 mins
🕐 Total Time: 30 mins

Servings per Recipe: 14
Calories	344 kcal
Fat	18 g
Carbohydrates	45g
Protein	3.9 g
Cholesterol	17 mg
Sodium	222 mg

Ingredients

18 C. popped popcorn
1 1/2 C. gumdrops
1 (10.5 oz.) package miniature marshmallows
1/2 C. butter
1 C. whole peanuts

Directions

1. Grease a 10-inch bundt pan.
2. In a bowl, add the popcorn, cashews and gumdrops and toss to coat.
3. Melt the marshmallow and butter completely and place the mixture over the popcorn mixture and stir to combine.
4. Transfer the mixture into the prepared pan and press firmly to smooth.
5. Refrigerate to chill before serving.

Outstanding Cake

Prep Time: 15 mins
Total Time: 1 hr 40 mins

Servings per Recipe: 12
Calories	283 kcal
Fat	11.1 g
Carbohydrates	42.5g
Protein	4.3 g
Cholesterol	62 mg
Sodium	479 mg

Ingredients

- cooking spray
- 1 (18.25 oz.) package white cake mix
- 1 C. canned pure pumpkin
- 1 (3.4 oz.) package instant butterscotch pudding mix
- 4 eggs, beaten
- 1/4 C. water
- 1/4 C. canola oil
- 2 tsp pumpkin pie spice

Directions

1. Set your oven to 250 degrees F before doing anything else and grease a 10-inch bundt pan.
2. In a large bowl, add the white cake mix, butterscotch pudding mix, pumpkin, eggs, water, canola oil and pumpkin pie spice and mix till well combined.
3. Transfer the mixture into the prepared pan and cook in the oven for about 60 minutes or till a toothpick inserted in the center comes out clean.
4. Let cake cool in the pan for 15 minutes before inverting onto a serving dish to remove cake from pan.

A CAKE
For Couples

Prep Time: 20 mins
Total Time: 30 mins

Servings per Recipe: 24
Calories	300 kcal
Fat	8.7 g
Carbohydrates	54.3g
Protein	4.2 g
Cholesterol	1 mg
Sodium	296 mg

Ingredients

1 (18.25 oz.) package chocolate cake mix
3 C. chocolate cookie crumbs
1 (16 oz.) package prepared chocolate frosting

1 (16 oz.) package gummi worms

Directions

1. Mix and bake the cake mix according to the package's directions into cupcake pans.
2. Let the cupcakes cool completely before the frosting.
3. Spread the chocolate icing over the cupcakes and sprinkle with the cookie crumbs.
4. Cut gummi worms in half and place the icing onto cut end of the worms and stick to the top of cupcakes.
5. Let the icing set for about 10 minutes before serving.

Elegant Mousse

Prep Time: 45 mins
Total Time: 4 hrs 46 mins

Servings per Recipe: 12
Calories 404 kcal
Fat 31.1 g
Carbohydrates 34g
Protein 3.2 g
Cholesterol 76 mg
Sodium 100 mg

Ingredients

- 1 C. chocolate cookie crumbs
- 3 tbsp butter, melted
- 2 pints fresh strawberries, halved
- 2 C. semisweet chocolate chips
- 1/2 C. water
- 2 tbsp light corn syrup
- 2 1/2 C. heavy cream, divided
- 1 tbsp white sugar

Directions

1. In a bowl, add the crumbs and butter and mix well.
2. In the bottom of a 9-inch spring form pan, place the mixture and press evenly.
3. Arrange strawberry halves around the pan side-by-side, pointed ends up, with cut sides against the side of the pan.
4. In a blender add the chocolate chips.
5. In a small pan, add the water and corn syrup and bring to a boil, then simmer for about 1 minute. Immediately pour over the chocolate chips and pulse till smooth.
6. Transfer into a bowl and keep aside to cool.
7. Meanwhile in another bowl, add 1 1/2 C. of the cream and beat till stiff peaks form.
8. With a rubber spatula fold about 1/3 of the whipped cream into the cooled chocolate mixture. Gently fold in the remaining whipped cream till the mixture is well combined.
9. Transfer the mousse into the prepared pan and smooth the top.
10. Cover with a plastic wrap and refrigerate for about 4-24 hours.
11. About 2 hours before the serving in a medium bowl, add the remaining 1/2 C. of the cream and beat till soft peaks form. Add the sugar and beat till stiff peaks form.
12. Remove the side of the spring form pan and place the cake on a serving plate.
13. Top the cake with the whipped cream and place the remaining halved strawberries over the whipped cream.

ETHAN'S
Favorite Cakes

Prep Time: 30 mins
Total Time: 1 hr 40 mins

Servings per Recipe: 24
Calories   131 kcal
Fat   7.6 g
Carbohydrates   14.5g
Protein   1.7 g
Cholesterol   4 mg
Sodium   57 mg

Ingredients

1 (12 oz.) package colored candy coating melts, divided
24 plain doughnut holes
24 lollipop sticks

1 tbsp multicolored candy sprinkles (jimmies)

Directions

1. In a small microwave-safe bowl, add about 1/4 C. of the candy melts and microwave at 40 percent power for about 30 seconds.
2. Stir the candy coating and microwave for about 30 second-intervals till the coating is melted.
3. With a lollipop stick, poke a hole halfway through a doughnut hole and then dip the end of the stick into the melted coating and reinsert into the hole.
4. This holds the doughnut hole firmly on the stick.
5. Stick the doughnut pop upright into a block of plastic foam and refrigerate for about 1 hour to set.
6. When pops are firmly attached to their sticks, in a small microwave-safe bowl, add the remaining candy melts and microwave at 40 percent power for about 30 seconds.
7. Stir the candy coating and microwave for about 30 second-intervals till the coating is melted.
8. Dip the doughnut hole into the coating, covering it completely.
9. Hold the dipped pop over a bowl, and sprinkle with colored candy sprinkles.
10. Return the decorated pops to the plastic foam block to set.

Valentine's Day Cake

Prep Time: 10 mins
Total Time: 55 mins

Servings per Recipe: 20
Calories   236 kcal
Fat   10.1 g
Carbohydrates   33.8g
Protein   2.8 g
Cholesterol   37 mg
Sodium   125 mg

Ingredients

- 1 C. margarine
- 1 1/2 C. white sugar
- 4 eggs
- 1 tsp almond extract
- 2 C. all-purpose flour
- 1 (21 oz.) can cherry pie filling
- 2 tbsp confectioners' sugar for dusting

Directions

1. Set your oven to 350 degrees F before doing anything else and grease and flour a 15x10-inch jellyroll pan.
2. In a large bowl, add the margarine and sugar and beat till fluffy and light.
3. Add the eggs, one at a time, beating continuously and then stir in the almond extract.
4. Slowly, add the flour and mix till well combined.
5. Transfer the mixture into the prepared pan and with the tip of a knife, mark squares in the mixture.
6. Place equal portions of the pie filling in the center of each square.
7. Cook in the oven for about 35-40 minutes or till a toothpick inserted in the center comes out clean.
8. Allow to cool, then dust with the confectioners' sugar.

SPECIAL
Summertime Mini Cakes

Prep Time: 45 mins
Total Time: 1 hr 35 mins

Servings per Recipe: 8
Calories	838 kcal
Fat	60.7 g
Carbohydrates	66.2g
Protein	9 g
Cholesterol	213 mg
Sodium	943 mg

Ingredients

3 1/2 C. self-rising flour
1/3 C. white sugar
1 tbsp ground cinnamon
1 1/4 C. chilled butter, cut into pieces
1 egg
3 1/2 C. whipped cream
1/4 C. milk
1 tbsp vanilla extract
2 tbsp white sugar
1 quart fresh strawberries, sliced
3 tbsp white sugar
2 C. whipped cream

Directions

1. Set your oven to 350 degrees F before doing anything else and line a baking sheet with the parchment paper.
2. In a large bowl, sift together the self-rising flour, 1/3 C. of the sugar and cinnamon.
3. With a pastry cutter, cut the cold butter and mix till a coarse crumb forms.
4. In another bowl, add the egg and whipped cream and beat well.
5. Add the cream mixture into the bowl of the flour mixture with the milk and vanilla extract and mix till a dough forms.
6. Place the dough onto a floured surface and knead for about 1 minute.
7. Spread the dough onto the prepared baking sheet and sprinkle with 2 tbsp of the sugar.
8. Cook in the oven for about 20 minutes. Let the cake to cool completely.
9. With a heart-shaped cookie cutter, cut out 16 hearts from the cake.
10. Carefully, remove the cut-outs.
11. In a bowl, mix together the strawberries and 3 tbsp of the sugar.
12. Arrange a shortcake heart on a plate and top with the sweetened strawberries.
13. Place about 2 tbsp of the whipped cream over the strawberries and top with another heart-shaped shortcake and serve.

Traditional German Cake

Prep Time: 30 mins
Total Time: 2 hrs 10 mins

Servings per Recipe: 12
Calories	693 kcal
Fat	33.6 g
Carbohydrates	88.8 g
Protein	6.4 g
Cholesterol	107 mg
Sodium	468 mg

Ingredients

- 1 2/3 C. all-purpose flour
- 2/3 C. unsweetened cocoa powder
- 1 1/2 tsp baking soda
- 1 tsp salt
- 1/2 C. shortening
- 1 1/2 C. white sugar
- 2 eggs
- 1 tsp vanilla extract
- 1 1/2 C. buttermilk
- 1/2 C. lemon lime soda
- 1/2 C. butter
- 3 1/2 C. confectioners' sugar
- 1 pinch salt
- 1 tsp strong brewed coffee
- 2 (14 oz.) cans pitted Bing cherries, drained
- 2 C. heavy whipping cream
- 1/2 tsp vanilla extract
- 1 tbsp lemon lime soda
- 1 (1 oz.) square semisweet chocolate

Directions

1. Set your oven to 350 degrees F before doing anything else and line the bottom of 2 (8-inch) round pans with the parchment papers.
2. In a large bowl, sift together the flour, cocoa powder, baking soda and 1 tsp of the salt.
3. In another bowl, add the shortening and sugar and beat till fluffy and light.
4. Add the eggs and vanilla and beat well.
5. Add the flour mixture, alternating with the buttermilk, beating till well combined.
6. Transfer the mixture into the prepared pans and cook in the oven for about 35-40 minutes or till a toothpick inserted in the center comes out clean.
7. Remove from the oven and keep aside to cool completely, then carefully, remove the parchment papers from the cakes.
8. Cut each layer in half, horizontally, making 4 layers total.
9. Sprinkle the layers with 1/2 C. of the lemon lime soda.
10. In a medium bowl, add the butter and beat till fluffy and light.

11. Add the confectioners' sugar, pinch of the salt, and coffee and beat till smooth. (If the mixture is too thick, stir in a couple tsp of the cherry juice or milk.)
12. Spread about 1/3 of the filling mixture over the first layer of the cake and top with about 1/3 of the cherries.
13. Repeat with the remaining layers.
14. In another bowl, add the cream and beat till stiff peaks form.
15. Add 1/2 tsp of the vanilla and 1 tbsp of the lemon lime soda and beat well.
16. Spread the frosting over the top and sides of the cake.
17. Sprinkle with chocolate curls made by using a potato peeler on semisweet baking chocolate.

ENJOY THE RECIPES?

KEEP ON COOKING
WITH 6 MORE FREE COOKBOOKS!

Visit our website and simply enter your email address to join the club and receive your 6 cookbooks.

http://booksumo.com/magnet

https://www.instagram.com/booksumopress/

https://www.facebook.com/booksumo/

Made in the USA
Coppell, TX
07 July 2020